Coastal Brown Bears In Valdez, Alaska Abercrombie Creek

Bob Benda

ISBN:1523838884
ISBN-13:978-1523838882

DEDICATION

Dedicated to people who enjoy watching and
photographing wildlife.

CONTENTS

ACKNOWLEDGMENTS

I thank my wife JoAnn for her patience and editorial skills.

Coastal brown bears den up for the winter in the mountains near Valdez. In late spring they emerge from their winter dens and start feeding on vegetation. When tourists visit Valdez they usually call them grizzly bears. Although they are the same species as grizzly bears they are called coastal brown bears, or brown bears. Grizzly bears live in interior Alaska. You can see them at Denali National Park. This photo shows a brown bear eating grass near Dayville road.

This is another coastal brown bear eating grass alongside Dayville Road. All species of bears are omnivores. This means they eat both plant and animal tissue.

When the salmon return to Valdez they spawn in the local streams. These are called wild salmon. Many of the salmon return to the Solomon Gulch Hatchery. These are called hatchery salmon. They were spawned, reared, and released into the ocean from the hatchery. The photos on pages 3 through 40 were all taken one day at Abercrombie Creek. This photo shows a female brown bear and her cub. The cub caught a salmon.

The cub took the salmon to shore to eat. Bear cubs start catching salmon in their second year. During the first year the mother bear catches the salmon and shares them with the cubs. By watching their mom the cubs learn how to catch salmon. Their mom prepares them to survive for when she eventually separates from them.

The mother bear walked out into the stream to look around. The cub started chasing another salmon near the shore.

The cub was successful and caught a pink salmon. The mother bear doesn't seem to be interested in what the cub is doing. This cub is probably in its third year with its mom. Because it's a single cub and late in the summer the mother bear might keep it for another winter. Occasionally brown bear cubs stay with their mother an extra year.

The cub has the salmon in its mouth and is walking toward the shore. You can see the red pieces of the last salmon the cub ate in the rocks. The mother bear is still just standing in the stream.

The cub is almost to the gravel shore where it ate the other salmon. Mom now seems to be interested in what the cub is doing. She may have decided she wants to share the salmon with the cub.

Mom must have decided to share the salmon with the cub. The seagulls are waiting around to eat any leftover pieces of salmon. The mother bear has a large belly. This indicates she has been eating enough fish to accumulate fat for her winter sleep.

The cub is finishing eating the salmon. Mom went back into the water. She's scratching her head with her hind leg.

The cub finished eating the salmon. Mom and the cub are both looking toward the brush. They looked like they may have heard something.

I guess they didn't hear or see anything. The cub started eating the last pieces of salmon. Mom is just standing there with her tongue hanging out.

Mom decided to walk back to the shore. The cub is following her. It looked like they might be leaving the area and going back into the woods.

When they reached the shore they turned around to look across the stream. The cub seems to be agitated by something. If there are other bears in the area the mother bear would be concerned. A male brown bear would be trouble for the mom and the cub.

The cub stood up behind the mother bear. It may be trying to get a better look across the stream. Other bears feed on the wild salmon swimming upstream so maybe the cub saw one.

Now the cub is using mom's back to support itself as it looks downstream. The mother bear is also looking downstream. They must have heard or seen something.

While the cub is looking upstream another brown bear walked into the stream. It must have been walking on the other side of the brush. The mother bear is just standing in the water with the cub leaning on her back.

The cub crouches down behind the mother bear and looks at the brown bear walking across the stream. This isn't an adult brown bear. It's probably an older cub.

The cub stands up again using mom for support. Mom has turned and is looking downstream at the smaller brown bear.

The smaller brown bear starts walking upstream. It's definitely an older brown bear cub. It may be a three year old that separated from its mother. Coastal brown bear females usually leave their cubs in the third year. Once the mother bear and cubs separate the female brown bear will mate again. She will give birth to her new cubs in the winter den.

Mom decides to leave the stream and walk into the brush. The cub follows her. They may stay in the brush until the other brown bear leaves the area. They may come back to feed later.

After mom and the cub left the stream an adult brown bear appeared on the other side of the brush. She must be the cub's mother. The other mom and cub must have sensed the other adult brown bear and left the area.

The other female brown bear and her cub start walking back downstream. She may have decided to leave the area and feed farther downstream.

After the mom and the older cub walked downstream another mother brown bear with two cubs walked out of the brush. They must have been in the woods on the far side of the stream. They may have been the reason the other brown bears left the area.

Another cub appeared so this mother brown bear probably had three cubs instead of two. I know there was a brown bear with four cubs near this area, but I never did see a fourth cub.

The mother brown bear with three cubs walked downstream out of sight. After a short time another smaller brown bear walked out of the brush close to where the mom and three cubs had been. Based on its size it's probably a juvenile brown bear.

The juvenile brown bear walked along the shore and started walking down the bank into the stream. It was the only bear in the area at this time.

It walked across the stream and started trying to catch a salmon. This is the same place the mother brown bear and her single cub were catching salmon before they went into the woods. If you notice there are no red salmon pieces left on the shore. The seagulls must have eaten them.

It caught a pink salmon by the tail. A seagull is watching it. The seagulls are always by the bears when they're feeding.

It looks like it's starting across the stream. It might carry the salmon to the other shore. The seagull keeps watching the brown bear.

It reached the other shore and walked toward the brush. Several times I have observed smaller bears take salmon into the woods to eat.

The brown bear walked back out of the brush. It must have finished eating the salmon. It's probably going back to try and catch another salmon.

The bear crossed the stream. It went back to the area where it caught the other salmon.

It chased the salmon upstream along the shore. The bear put its head under the water trying to catch it.

The salmon must have gotten away from the bear. The bear continued chasing it along the gravel shoreline. You can see the salmon by the bear's mouth.

The salmon must have escaped again, but this juvenile brown bear doesn't seem to want to give up. It's splashing water everywhere trying to get the fish. The question is will the salmon or the brown bear be successful?

The brown bear was successful. It caught a female pink salmon. You can see the orange colored eggs being squeezed out of the fish. Bears lick up the eggs after they eat the fish. The eggs are an important part of the bears diet. They are beneficial to the bear for storing fat for the winter sleep.

While the juvenile brown bear was catching its salmon the mother brown bear and its cub came back to the stream. They were both watching the juvenile brown bear cross the stream to eat its catch.

It looked like mom and the cub were looking at something upstream. The cub seemed more agitated than the mother bear.

Whatever it was they decided to leave the area again instead of trying to catch more salmon. I was able to take all the photos at Abercrombie Creek in about two hours. I saw more brown bear adults and cubs this time than I ever saw before in my years photographing bears in Valdez. It was exciting to watch and photograph all the brown bear activity.

ALASKA COASTAL BROWN BEAR FACTS

1. Alaska coastal bears are called "brown bears".
2. Alaska inland and lower 48 States brown bears are called "grizzly bears".
3. The largest Alaska coastal brown bears are in the Kodiak archipelago islands.
4. A male brown bear is called a boar.
5. A female brown bears is called a sow
6. Brown bears standing on their hind legs are 6-7 feet. Kodiak bears can be over 10 feet.
7. Male brown bears are larger than females (sexual dimorphism).
8. Adult males weigh 300-850 pounds while adult females weigh 200-450 pounds.
9. Kodiak bears can weigh over 1,000 pounds.
10. Brown bears are omnivorous eating grass, berries, mosses, small animals and fish.
11. They prepare for their winter sleep by eating up to 90 pounds of food a day during summer.
12. They gain up to 3 pounds/day of body fat to prepare for sleeping during the winter.
13. Bears will wake up during the winter. They do not enter true hibernation, but deep sleep.
14. Brown bears live 20 to 25 years in the wild.
15. Brown bears mature at 5 years. Males and females are solitary except during mating.

16. The female gives birth in the den during the winter sleep.

17. Typically they give birth to two cubs, but can have up to four cubs.

18. The cubs stay with the mother for 2 to 4 years, depending on when she mates again.

19. Female brown bears have been observed adopting orphaned cubs. This rarely happens, but has been observed twice in Alaska. Once at Katmai National Park and Preserve in September 2014 and years ago on Kodiak Island. Alaska Dispatch News September 16, 2014 "Supermom' grizzly adopts yearling www.ADN.com .

20. The cubs have to avoid the male brown bears during the mating season. The female brown bear and the cubs usually separate at this time. This usually occurs during their third year together.

21. Additional facts can be found at:
http:/www.pbs.org/wnet/nature/episodes/bears

ABOUT THE AUTHOR

Bob Benda is a retired college Professor of Biology. He worked for two years in East Africa on a Lake Victoria fisheries project. He also worked for the US Fish and Wildlife Service and the US Forest Service. During the EXXON Valdez oil spill he worked for the Alaska Department of Environmental Conservation. He also participated in oil spill damage assessment. He taught oiled wildlife capture, stabilization, and transportation workshops. Watching and photographing wildlife is his hobby.

www.ingramcontent.com/pod-product-compliance
Lightning Source LLC
Chambersburg PA
CBHW040326010626
45792CB00024B/2169